WR READER®

LEARNING LIBRARY

LIFE LONG AGO

Ancient Greece

by Tea Benduhn

Reading consultant: Susan Nations, M.Ed.,
author/literacy coach/consultant in literacy development

Please visit our web site at: www.garethstevens.com
For a free color catalog describing Weekly Reader® Early Learning Library's list
of high-quality books, call 1-877-445-5824 (USA) or 1-800-387-3178 (Canada).
Weekly Reader® Early Learning Library's fax: (414) 336-0164.

Library of Congress Cataloging-in-Publication Data

Benduhn, Tea.
    Ancient Greece / by Tea Benduhn.
       p. cm. — (Life long ago)
    Includes bibliographical references and index.
    ISBN-13: 978-0-8368-7782-3 (lib. bdg.)
    ISBN-13: 978-0-8368-7787-8 (softcover)
    1. Greece—Civilization—To 146 B.C.—Juvenile literature. 2. Greece—
Social life and customs—Juvenile literature. I. Title.
DF78.B39   2007
938—dc22
                                        2006030345

This edition first published in 2007 by
Weekly Reader® Early Learning Library
A Member of the WRC Media Family of Companies
330 West Olive Street, Suite 100
Milwaukee, WI 53212 USA

Managing editor: Valerie J. Weber
Art direction: Tammy West
Cover design, page layout, and illustrations: Dave Kowalski
Picture research: Diane Laska-Swanke

Picture credits: Cover, title, © Roger Wood/CORBIS; pp. 4, 7, 10, 13, 17, 18 © The Granger Collection, New York; pp. 5, 11 Dave Kowalski/© Weekly Reader Early Learning Library; p. 6 © North Wind Picture Archives; pp. 8, 16 © Bettmann/CORBIS; pp. 9, 15 © C. M. Dixon/Ancient Art & Architecture Collection; p. 12 © G. Tortoli/Ancient Art & Architecture Collection; pp. 14, 19, 20 © Ronald Sheridan/Ancient Art & Architecture Collection; p. 21 © Blue Lantern Studio/CORBIS

Printed in the United States of America

1 2 3 4 5 6 7 8 9 10 10 09 08 07 06

TABLE OF CONTENTS

Cover and Title Page: The Acropolis served as the center of activity for the people of Athens in ancient Greece.

CHAPTER 1

Who Were the Ancient Greeks?

Have you heard the story about a boy who cried wolf? What about the story about the tortoise winning the race against the hare? If you have, then you already know a little bit about the ancient Greeks. A Greek writer named Aesop wrote these fables.

Aesop told many stories about animals and people during his lifetime from 620 to 650 B.C.

The ancient Greeks lived about three thousand years ago in an area along the Mediterranean Sea. Ancient Greece had many small islands. The soil was too rocky for good farming, and most people fished for food.

The mainland of ancient Greece shared a border with southern Europe. Many Greeks also lived on islands in the Ionian and Aegean Seas.

Europe

Greece

Aegean Sea

Ionian Sea

Athens

Mediterranean Sea

Sea of Crete

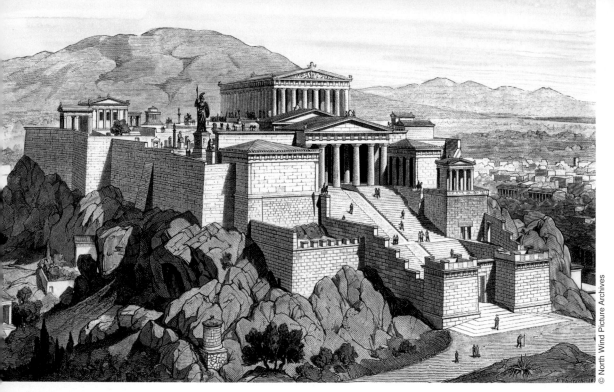

The main building of the Acropolis, called the Parthenon, was the center of Greek government in Athens.

People all over ancient Greece spoke the same language. They also worshipped the same gods. They did not, however, share the same rulers. Ancient Greece was made up of many different **city-states**. Each city-state had its own government.

Sparta and Athens were two of the most important city-states. They often fought each other. Sparta was famous for its great army. Athens was famous for its arts and sciences. In 146 B.C., Romans conquered both areas and the rest of Greece, ending the Greek Empire.

Armed only with spears, shields, and helmets, armies from each city-state fought for control of land.

7

CHAPTER 2

Greek Government and Gods

Kings ruled some city-states, such as Sparta. Many other city-states, such as Athens, were **democracies**. **Citizens** in democracies elected their rulers. Most people in ancient Greece, however, were not allowed to be citizens. Women, children, slaves, and people born in other places were not allowed to vote.

In ancient Greece, some people, such as prisoners of war, were sold as slaves.

People living in Athens focused on education. Many people learned to read and write. They also developed arts, such as painting and poetry. They even carved sculptures out of marble.

People in Athens created large, life-size statues. The statues often represented goddesses, gods, and perfect humans.

In Sparta, everyone had to be strong and healthy. When a baby was born, soldiers came to the house to check the baby. If it was not healthy, they took the infant and left it to die on a hillside. At the age of seven, boys went to the army barracks to start military training. The Spartan army was feared through all of Greece.

When they were not fighting, Spartan soldiers exercised to stay in shape.

Ancient Greeks believed their many gods lived at the top of Mount Olympus, which was the highest point in Greece. Zeus was the king of gods, Athena was born from his head, and Apollo was Zeus's son.

The gods and goddesses watched over different parts of daily life.

Gods	Goddesses
Apollo: light, poetry, music	**Aphrodite:** love, beauty
Ares: war	**Artemis:** hunting, wildlife
Hephaestus: craftsmanship	**Athena:** wisdom, war, Athens
Hermes: business, messages	**Demeter:** farming
Poseidon: sea and earthquakes	**Hera:** marriage (wife of Zeus)
Zeus: king of gods and sky	**Hestia:** family and hearth

3

Daily Life in Ancient Greece

The ancient Greeks built their houses of sun-dried mud bricks. Most homes were built around an open courtyard. In Athens, women were expected to stay indoors. In Sparta, however, women had more freedom to leave home. Their husbands were often away, fighting wars.

For thousands of years, ancient Greeks built their homes in similar ways. These ruins are about 4,000 years old.

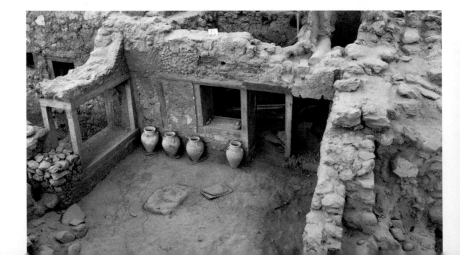

Girls usually got married by the time they were fourteen years old. Their fathers picked their husbands for them. Men fought in the army or worked on their education until their late twenties. They usually waited until they were thirty or older to get married.

A jar for make-up from 400 B.C. shows a Greek bride and groom riding in a carriage pulled by horses.

Many families wanted to have sons to fight in the army. In Sparta, soldiers spent most of their lives with other soldiers. They ate, slept, lived, and trained with the army even after they were married. Military service did not end for Spartan men until they reached the age of sixty.

This bronze statue shows a Spartan soldier dressed for battle.

In all city-states, most girls stayed at home to learn cooking, weaving, and housekeeping from their mothers. Some boys in Athens or other city-states were allowed to go to school. They learned reading, writing, math, geography, sports, and public speaking.

In this carving, a child learns to read from a teacher.

15

Men and women wore similar clothes to each other. Men sometimes wore shorter tunics, however.

The clothing of the ancient Greeks changed little over hundreds of years. The Greeks disapproved of difference. Men, women, children, and people of all classes wore a **tunic** fastened with a brooch. They covered themselves with a cloak.

Ancient Greeks ate their main meal late in the day. Meals included cheese, vegetables, and seafood such as octopus and squid. They picked up food with their fingers and used flat bread as a spoon. Wealthy people ate while lying on couches and often had a party after the meal. Sometimes, women played songs and danced for the men.

Ancient Greek pottery shows a party with music after a feast.

In the sixth century B.C., the Greeks discovered that disease could be cured by medicine. A doctor named Hippocrates developed a way to figure out a patient's problems that doctors still use today.

An ancient Greek doctor treats a patient. Doctors today must take an oath named after Hippocrates. They must promise to heal people as well as they can.

The Greeks developed many of the science and math ideas that you learn in school today. Some of the world's greatest advice comes from the Greeks, too. Next time you hear "slow and steady wins the race," you may think of Aesop's fables and the ancient Greeks!

The Tortoise and the Hare is one of Aesop's fables. The tortoise wins their race because he kept going, no matter what happened.

GLOSSARY

barracks — training grounds and housing for the army

brooch — jeweled pin for decoration and for pinning clothes

citizens — people who live in an area and are allowed to make decisions about that area

city-states — cities and the lands surrounding them that have their own governments

cloak — cape

courtyard — an open, outdoor yard with a building surrounding it

craftsmanship — the skilled production of items

democracies — governments ruled by leaders who are chosen by the people

fables — stories with a lesson at the end

fastened — pinned together

geography — the study of maps and lands

Olympic games — a series of many sporting events in which several countries compete to win the gold medal

tunic — a long piece of clothing like a long shirt

FOR MORE INFORMATION

Books

Ancient Greece. DK Eyewitness Books (series). Anne Pearson (DK Publishing)

Ancient Greeks. Ancient Civilizations (series). Anita Ganeri (Compass Point Books)

The Best Book of Ancient Greece. The Best Book of (series). Belinda Weber (Kingfisher)

Kids in Ancient Greece. Kids Throughout History (series). Lisa A. Wroble (PowerKids Press)

Web Site

History for Kids: Ancient Greece

www.historyforkids.org/learn/greeks/index.htm
Find out about the art ancient Greeks made, the sports they played, and more.

INDEX

About the Author

Tea Benduhn writes and edits books for children and teens. Her book reviews, author interviews, and articles have appeared in magazines and newspapers. She lives in the beautiful state of Wisconsin.

24